TIME FOR KIDS READERS

Close-Up On Tonga

by Aaron Derr

Harcourt

Orlando Austin Chicago New York Toronto London San Diego

Visit *The Learning Site!*
www.harcourtschool.com

The Kingdom of Tonga

The Kingdom of Tonga is the first country in the world to see each new day. For example, if you had been there on New Year's Eve 1999, you would have been one of the first people to welcome the new year.

This is a modern version of a double-hulled canoe. Visitors to Tonga can take day trips on boats like it.

Tonga is a group of islands in the South Pacific about two-thirds of the way between Hawaii and New Zealand. The kingdom is made up of 170 islands, but only 36 of them have people living on them. Of the 106,000 people who live in Tonga today, more than half of them live on the island of Tongatapu. Known as the Friendly Islands, tourism is one of the major sources of income for the nation today.

Tonga is to the east of Australia.

Although no one knows for certain where Tonga's original settlers came from, it is believed that they may have come from Fiji about 3,500 years ago. These early seafarers traveled in large double-hulled canoes, settled on the islands, and formed tribes. The different chiefs would often fight each other for land.

British explorers who began visiting Tonga in 1773 had strong influences on Tongan government. In fact, it was the British explorer Captain James Cook who first named Tonga the Friendly Islands, because of the warm welcome he received from the native peoples. In 1875 a constitutional monarchy was formed and is still the government that exists today. This means that there is a king, but that representatives to a national assembly are elected by its citizens.

Cook hails the British flag raised on his visit to Tonga.

Tonga Traditions

Every celebration and every holiday in Tonga is sure to include dancing. Tonga's traditional dance is the *lakalaka*. The *lakalaka* is a graceful dance, using careful movements of the hands and feet. More than 200 people can dance the *lakalaka* at one time. Sometimes as many as 1,000 people perform it. The dancers also sing each story, retelling a legend or an episode of Tonga's history.

Tongans are proud of their history and often dress in traditional clothing.

Tongans use music and dance to tell traditional stories.

Singing was the Tongans' main form of music in the past. They also played some instruments that may seem unusual to people in other parts of the world. One, the *fangufangu,* is a flute that was played with the nose. It's made from a piece of bamboo with six holes cut in it. To play it, a musician placed one end to one of his or her nostrils and blocked the other nostril with the thumb. Today few people actually play the *fangufangu*. Most of the flutes that are left are in museums.

A *kele'a* is a trumpet made from a large conch, a kind of seashell. The *kele'a* is still used today. It is sometimes blown as a signal to gather people together. But it can also be used to make music. *Kele'a* orchestras have many players and are organized the way a chorus of singers would be. Each orchestra has groups of bass, soprano, tenor, and alto *kele'a*.

Ngatu is a kind of fabric made from tree bark. It is made by women who beat the bark over logs. The women drum on the bark rhythmically as they work.

Fakatangi songs are fables or tales set to music. Tongans recite them at family gatherings. As the storyteller gets to the turning point in the plot, he or she sings the *fakatangi* song that goes with the story. *Hiva kakala* means "fragrant songs," and are love songs usually sung by a group of men. A dance called the *tau'olunga* is done to the music of a *hiva kakala*.

Music, always important to Tongans, is especially so on Sundays. More than a hundred years ago, most people on Tonga became Christians. Churchgoing remains a Sunday tradition. On Tonga, this means going to church not once, but up to three times on Sunday. The hymns have their roots not only in Christianity but also in the traditional songs of Tonga.

Ngatu is used for clothing and as paper.

For hundreds of years, Tongans have made a kind of cloth called ngatu from mulberry tree bark. The bark is laid over logs, and then beaten and brushed, which is hard work. "It is very hard on your arms," Princess Salote Pilolevu Tuita says. But she adds, "Ngatu making can be fun." Along with 200 other women, the princess created a large cloth from ngatu for the birthday of her father, King Taufa'ahau Tupou IV.

In the past, Tongans drew pictures on ngatu to record their history. There are old ngatu pictures of Halley's Comet, which can be seen from Earth every 76 years. There are also ngatu pictures of fighter planes from World War II.

Ngatu used to be common in many islands in the South Pacific. It was once used in places such as Hawaii, Tahiti, and Samoa. Today the people of those other islands use it mainly for tourist souvenirs. But in Tonga, ngatu is still used everywhere.

The "royal tortoise" strolls the grounds of the monarch's palace.

Feasting is a major pastime on Tonga. The feasts are also famous throughout the Pacific. Huge amounts of food are served on a *pola*, a huge tray. Each *pola* holds up to 30 different kinds of food. Favorite foods are steamed pork, fish, crayfish, beef, octopus, and many different kinds of tropical fruits.

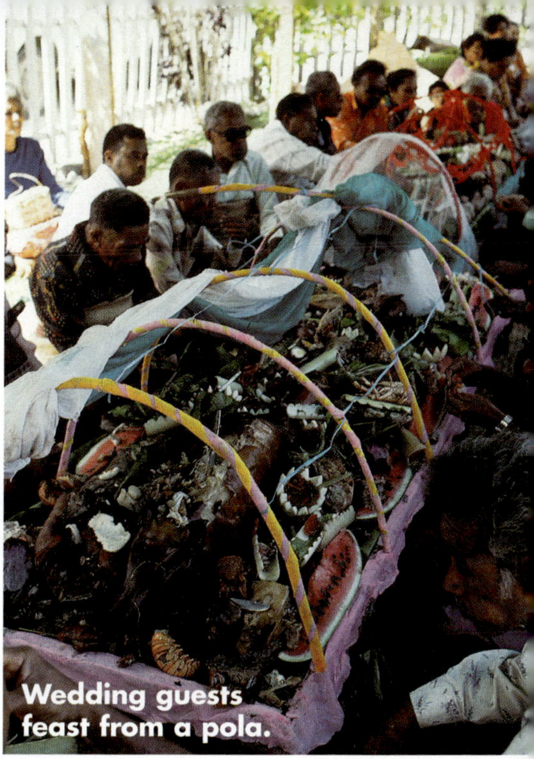

Wedding guests feast from a pola.

Taufa'ahau Tupou IV became king of Tonga in 1965. He is shown here with his wife, Queen Mata'aho.

Tourists come to Tonga for the sunsets, the beaches, the warm weather, and the Tongan people.

Tourism

One thing Tongans don't cut back on is friendliness. Visitors to the islands almost always remark on how friendly the people of Tonga are. Judy Meyer, a travel agent who has organized many trips to Tonga, says that the islands really deserve their nickname, the Friendly Islands. "They're just great," says Meyer of Tonga's people. "And they really welcome visitors."

A tourist who wants to visit Tonga must first fly to Hawaii, Fiji, or New Zealand. The next step is to take a much smaller plane to Fua'amotu International Airport on Tonga's largest island, Tongatapu. Although about 170 islands make up the country, most are very small. Added together, the total area of the country would be only about four times the size of Washington, D.C.

Because Tonga is harder to get to than some other island countries in the Pacific, it isn't as developed. Tongatapu has about 20 hotels. In contrast, the islands of Hawaii, some of which are tourist destinations, have thousands of hotels.

Flying foxes hang by their feet from trees.

Each block of the Ha'amonga Trilathon weighs more than 40 tons.

Tonga was the first South Pacific nation to create national parks and reserves to protect its environment. Visitors can explore deep limestone caves or see flying foxes—large fruit-eating bats. Or they can visit the Ha'amonga Trilathon. These three giant blocks of stone are set up like an arch or gateway. Two blocks form the side, and the third rests across it. The arrangement stands about 15 feet (5 m) tall and was built around A.D. 1200. Why was it built? How did the builders get the stones in place? The answer, it is often said, is lost in the mists of time.

What's the big attraction on Tonga? The beaches, of course! They are unspoiled and beautiful. No giant hotels are lined up to spoil the view of sand, trees, and blue-green water as far as the eye can see.

TFK Spotlight

Tonga is a tiny nation, which makes it hard for it to be competitive in world sports events. But Tonga does have one Olympic Games medal winner. He is boxer Paea Wolfgram, who won a silver medal in the 1996 Summer Olympics. Wolfgram is Tonga's biggest athlete in more ways than one. He weighed 309 pounds (140 kg) when he competed in 1996! No one expected him to get far at the Olympics—least of all himself. "I'm just a mild-mannered clerk," he told reporters.

Wolfgram surprised the world when he beat Alexis Rubalcaba in an Olympic boxing match. Rubalcaba was from Cuba, which usually produces great boxers. Rubalcaba was said to be one of the best fighters in the world. But because he had never seen Wolfgram train or fight, he didn't know what to expect.

Wolfgram shocked Rubalcaba with his quick footwork. As soon as the ringside crowd realized that Wolfgram had a chance to win, onlookers started chanting "Tonga! Tonga!"

Next, Wolfgram fought against an awesome opponent from the Ukraine for the gold medal, but lost. It didn't matter. The fact that he had won a silver medal was a great accomplishment. When he returned to Tonga he received a hero's welcome.

Not only are the beaches uncrowded and clean, but so is the water. Scuba diving, sailing, and fishing are all popular pastimes. The waters around Tonga are filled with coral reefs. A coral reef looks like colorful rock, but it's actually made up of millions of tiny animals. The animals leave hard deposits, sort of like a seashell, that form the reef. The reefs around Tonga are home to more than 100 kinds of fish.

A gorgonian sea fan grows from an underwater cliff. Divers must be careful not to touch the delicate fan.

The waters around Tonga are also home to some of the world's largest animals—humpback whales. Every year, hundreds of people from around the world come to Tonga for whale watching. Humpback whales spend most of the year eating and fattening up near Antarctica, around the South Pole. From June until November, the whales travel thousands of miles to an area near Tonga. There they mate and give birth to their young in the warm waters.

Whales travel to the warmer water to give birth because their young can't handle the cold water. The only problem is that there isn't much food in the Tongan waters for the adult whales to eat. Once the young gain enough fat to stay warm, the whales head back south to the Antarctic.

People used to hunt and kill the whales that were coming to the Tongan waters. The whales almost reached extinction. In 1979, the kingdom made it illegal to hunt the mammals. Now people come just to watch these amazing animals. There's plenty to look at! Adult humpback whales are huge. They can weigh up to 40 tons. Humpbacks are also unique because of the sounds they make. The whales seem to communicate with sounds that are much like songs. The different kinds of sounds are repeated in patterns, just as in a song. Though scientists have studied these sounds for years, they still aren't sure exactly what purpose the sounds serve.

Tonga Today

In one way at least, Tonga is on the cutting edge of technology. It's the electronic "home" of thousands of sites on the World Wide Web. In 1993, a business executive named Eric Gullichsen, who was in Tonga on vacation, had an idea. Gullichsen was involved with the Internet. He realized that a country like Tonga could make a lot of money by setting up its own domain on the World Wide Web.

Every address on the Web is part of a domain, a group of addresses. The end of each Web address tells the domain to which it belongs. The United States has domains, including *.com*, *.net*, and *.org*. If, for example, Jane Doe wants to name her Web site "JaneDoe," she has to make it janedoe.com, janedoe.net, or janedoe.org. If those three are taken, Jane would have to find a different Web name.

Eric Gullichsen knew that the names for Web sites were being used up quickly and that some people were willing to pay a lot of money for names they wanted. "There's nothing magical about the letters *dot com*," Eric told TIME magazine. "Why not use *dot to* for Tonga?"

Gullichsen met with Tonga's Crown Prince Tupouto'a to explain his idea. They agreed to create TONIC, the Tongan Network Information Center. A computer at the Tongan consulate in San Francisco is used to route Internet sites with *.to* in their names. The result: many Web sites now end with Tonga's *.to*. This has not only brought money into the kingdom but has also brought Tonga into the Information Age.

Tonga's government continues to pursue new businesses and more tourists. What will the future bring? Will more tourists discover Tonga? Will the Internet turn it into a small financial powerhouse? People who know the country hope that as Tonga ventures further into the twenty-first century, it will hold on to the beauty of its beaches, the purity of its waters, and, especially, the uniquely special quality of its people.

Eric Gullichsen, Web executive

Y2K Tonga

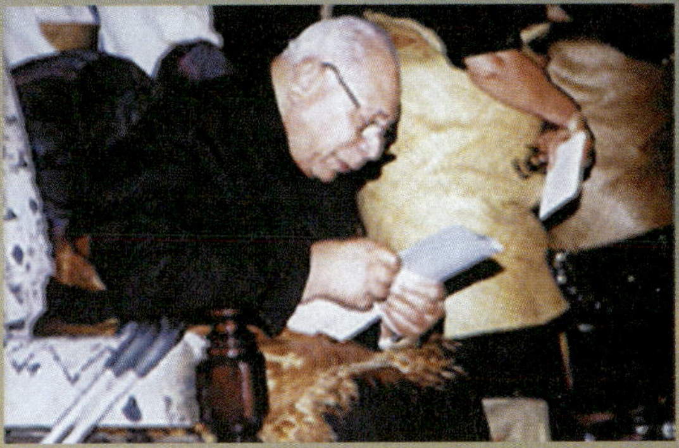

Tonga's monarch leads a prayer for peace and health in the new century.

Where was the best place to be when 1999 turned to 2000? Tonga! Tonga was the first land to officially experience the new millennium. For example, sunrise on January 1, 2000, came to Tonga 17 hours before it came to the United States.

Many people traveled to Tonga to be the first to experience the new century. To celebrate, Tongan children lined up along the shore with lighted torches. Tonga also hosted feasts, cultural shows, sports events, parades, and festivals to celebrate the new century.

TFK

About Tonga

- Tonga is made up of 170 islands, but people live on only 36 of them.
- Most Tongans are Polynesian. Polynesia is a group of Pacific islands that includes Hawaii.
- English is one of the official languages of Tonga. The native language is Tongan.
- The king of Tonga has four children including the Crown Prince, who will become king when his father dies.